ANIMAL LIVES

The Barn Owl

KINGFISHER
Larousse Kingfisher Chambers Inc.
95 Madison Avenue
New York, New York 10016

First published in 1999
10 9 8 7 6 5 4 3 2 1
1(TR)/1198/SC/NEW(NEW)/150NYM

LIBRARY OF CONGRESS CATALOGING-IN-PUBLICATION DATA
Kitchen, Bert.
The barn owl / illustrated by Bert Kitchen; written by Sally
Tagholm.—1st ed.
p.   cm.—(Animal lives)
Includes index.
Summary: Describes the physical characteristics, hunting, feeding,
nesting, mating, and molting of the barn owl, as well as the nine
different species.
1. Barn owl—Juvenile literature. [1. Barn owl. 2. Owls.]
I. Tagholm, Sally. II. Title. III. Series: Animal lives (New York,
N.Y.)
QL596.S85K58   1999
598.9'7—dc21   98–39797   CIP   AC

Editor: Christian Lewis
Series editor: Miranda Smith
Series designer: Sarah Goodwin

ISBN 0-7534-5171-9

Printed in Hong Kong

ANIMAL LIVES
The Barn Owl

Illustrated by
Bert Kitchen

Written by
Sally Tagholm

KING*f*ISHER

NEW YORK

The barn owl sits motionless on the gate, a ghostly shape in the slowly gathering dusk. The winter fields are frozen, the trees bare, and the landscape deserted. Small creatures, such as long-tailed field mice, do not stray far from home. With food so hard to find, the owl will have to leave his favorite patch tonight. The pale sun has almost disappeared from view. It is time to hunt.

He swoops slowly over the trees and hedges, across the rolling countryside, leaving the gate far behind. A silent phantom, his huge wings quietly beat the night air, their soft downy surface deadening the sound. Under the splendid feathers, his body is slim and surprisingly light—the perfect flying machine. With his superefficient sense of hearing, and big, round eyes that can see in the dark, he will find a plump mouse or juicy rat before long. He might even come across a flock of small birds roosting in some frosty hedge.

The barn owl slows down and almost comes to a halt. He has found what he is looking for. He hovers, suspended in the dark night air. With his eyes fixed on the small brown mouse perched on a fallen tree trunk, he bides his time. Suddenly he plunges, snatching his prey, folding it into the viselike grip of his deadly claws. He flies off triumphantly, his prize hanging from his beak.

Spring is here, the
trees are
in bloom, and
small creatures scurry and
scamper after the long, cold
winter. After months of
roosting alone, the barn
owl has found a mate.
From his perch on the gate,
his bloodcurdling screech
pierces the still night air.
The female answers, and
they twist and turn in the
air, calling to each other,
and playing tag in the dark,
like ghostly acrobats.

Now there is plenty of food in the hedges and ditches, and the owl does not have to fly far to find a tasty, long-tailed field mouse. He presents it to the female, a juicy offering which she swallows whole. Then he flies off again in search of more food—the more the better. The female encourages him, begging for food by making husky hisses that sound a little like snoring. Sometimes, the male hovers in front of her in midair, fluttering his powerful wings. After she fully accepts him it will be time to mate.

The two owls
roost together
in the crumbling
buildings of the deserted
farm. One of their favorite
places is the old barn. It
has a special "owl window"
high up under the gable,
built long ago when
farmers needed owls
to hunt the rats and mice
that ate their grain. It is
peaceful and dark up in the
rafters—the perfect place
to nest. The birds preen
each other in the shadows.

After mating, the female lays a clutch of five smooth, white eggs, one at a time. This happens over ten days and she warms them by sitting tight on her nest in the gloom above some forgotten bales of straw and rusty farm machinery. She only goes off duty occasionally to preen and stretch her wings out in the open air. At regular intervals she stands up and turns the eggs to make sure they are heated evenly, pushing them around with her face and bill. They soon get a little dirty because the nest is really just a layer of dry old owl pellets—the scattered fur, feathers, and tiny bones of undigested prey. The remains of several small rodents, brought in by the male to feed his mate weeks ago, lie rotting in the nearby straw.

The barn owl is very busy hunting in the fields, bringing back his catches to his hungry mate. This time it is a short-tailed vole—the barn owl's favorite food. The days go slowly by and she sits patiently on the eggs, hardly moving. After four long weeks, the brooding female becomes restless. At last, she can hear faint, cheeping calls coming from inside her first egg.

Tiny cracks appear on the shell as the first chick gets ready to leave his safe, warm world. He has a special bump on top of his beak—an egg tooth—to help him push his way out. Blind and helpless, his scrawny pink body unfolds like a tiny dinosaur. Two days later, a second egg hatches. The mother feeds her new chicks with scraps torn from freshly delivered prey. By the time the last egg hatches, the first chick is ten days old and his eyes are about to open.

W ith so many mouths to feed, the male hunts before dusk and after dawn, as well as at night. He brings in the odd frog or little bird, and a constant supply of small mammals. The chicks' bodies are soon covered with fluffy white down, and their newly opened eyes are black and beady. As they grow, their mother also spreads her wings, leaving the nest to hunt.

As their beautiful speckled grown-up feathers appear, the five owlets slowly lose their white baby fluff. They explore the nest, hopping around over the squashed pellets, their heads bobbing from side to side as they investigate in the gloom. Fearless, they soon search out every nook and cranny of the hayloft and peer through the old round window at the world outside. By now, the mother roosts away from the barn, coming back only to deliver fresh food supplies. One by one, the young owls start to exercise their brand new wings. They experiment, stretching and flapping, preparing for their first perilous flights. After almost two months, the first-hatched flies from the nest. His brothers and sisters soon follow.

I t has been a long, hot summer, and the farmers have finished bringing in the crops. The earth is baked hard and dusty under a sea of stubble. The fields are full of small, scuttling creatures that are easy targets for a pair of sharp claws. All five owlets are safely fledged. The barn owl and his mate, who only have themselves to feed now, sit quietly on the gate under a clear, moonlit sky.

THE BARN OWL

Scientific name: *Tyto alba.*

Nicknames: Screech owl, monkey-faced owl.

Size: Male and female birds are about the same size, measuring about 16–18 inches from head to tail. Wingspan is about 44 inches.

Weight: Males usually weigh about 14 ounces. Females weigh about 18 ounces in the breeding season and 16 ounces in winter.

Distribution: Worldwide. Barn owls are found on every continent except the polar regions, although they avoid mountainous regions, cold areas, very hot desert regions, and dense tropical forests.

Habitat: Open or lightly wooded country, grasslands, and cultivated areas, as well as cities.

Prey: Small mammals, particularly voles, as well as rats, shrews, mice, frogs, and small birds.

Nests: Abandoned buildings, barns, church towers, holes in trees.

Eggs: Laid in early or late spring, depending on food supply. Second clutches are sometimes laid in summer. Minimum number of eggs: 2. Maximum number of eggs: 9. The eggs take about 31 days to hatch.

Near relatives: The grass owl (southern Africa), the sooty owl (New Guinea and Australia), and the masked owl (Indonesia and Australia).

BARN OWLS IN THE COUNTRY

Barn owls normally keep well out of sight, flying by night and roosting in quiet, undisturbed places during the day. However, it is sometimes possible to see one hunting on a wintry day, or carrying prey back to its young at dusk or dawn in midsummer. You may even catch a glimpse of a barn owl in the headlights of a car at night. Keep an eye out for shiny, black pellets or pale, molted feathers in old farm buildings, but never approach or disturb the birds, particularly when they are nesting.

CONSERVATION

Although it was found all over the world in the past, the barn owl is now a rare and endangered bird. Its numbers have declined dramatically this century as farmers have cleared land to make gigantic fields to produce more and more food. The barn owl's natural hunting grounds are vanishing as hedges, ditches, and rough grasslands disappear. Their nesting sites are in danger, too, as hollow trees are cut down and old buildings demolished or converted. Barn owl conservation groups have begun to take action, preserving the rough grasslands, which are rich in prey, and providing nest boxes.

BARN OWL WORDS

bill a bird's beak

brooding sitting on eggs to keep them warm and hatch them

clutch a group of eggs laid at one time

down a bird's soft baby feathers

egg tooth the bump on the top of a baby owl's beak that it uses to break out of its shell during hatching

fledged fully feathered and able to fly

mammal an animal that produces milk to feed its young

pellet a dried mass of undigested food such as bones and fur

preen to trim and clean feathers with the beak

prey an animal or bird that is hunted for food

rodent an animal such as a rat or a mouse, which is hunted as prey by the barn owl

roost a place for perching or resting

screech the barn owl's harsh scream

FOR FURTHER INFORMATION

The National Audobon Society
700 Broadway
New York, NY 10003
(212) 979 3000
www.audobon.org

A Bird's-eye View
(The ABA's student newsletter)
41a Dudley Street
Arlington, MA 02174
(617) 641 1769
birdseyevu@aol.com

American Birding Association (ABA)
P.O. Box 6599
Colorado Springs, CO 80934
(719) 578 1614
member@aba.org

Eton Birding Society
P.O. Box 928
Geneva, NY 14456
(315) 781 0465
hic1@cornell.edu

INDEX

ACKNOWLEDGMENTS

*The author and publishers are grateful for the help and advice that David Ramsden
of the Barn Owl Trust (U.K.) has given them in the preparation of this book.*